WHAT YOU DIDN'T KNOW ABOUT HISTORY

Life in the
WILD WEST

By Arthur K. Britton

Gareth Stevens
Publishing

Please visit our website, www.garethstevens.com. For a free color catalog of all our high-quality books, call toll free 1-800-542-2595 or fax 1-877-542-2596.

Library of Congress Cataloging-in-Publication Data

Britton, Arthur K.
 Life in the wild West / Arthur K. Britton.
     p. cm. — (What you didn't know about history)
 Includes index.
 ISBN 978-1-4339-8440-2 (pbk.)
 ISBN 978-1-4339-8441-9 (6-pack)
 ISBN 978-1-4339-8439-6 (library binding)
 1. West (U.S.)—History—Juvenile literature. 2. Frontier and pioneer life—West (U.S.)—Juvenile literature. I. Title.
 F591.B8525 2013
 978—dc23
                                        2012022059

First Edition

Published in 2013 by
Gareth Stevens Publishing
111 East 14th Street, Suite 349
New York, NY 10003

Copyright © 2013 Gareth Stevens Publishing

Designer: Dan Hosek and Michael J. Flynn
Editor: Kristen Rajczak

Photo credits: Cover, pp. 1, 5 Superstock/Getty Images; p. 7 Pictorial Parade/
Archive Photos/Getty Images; pp. 9, 11 Buyenlarge/Archive Photos/Getty Images;
p. 13 Transcendental Graphics/Archive Photos/Getty Images; p. 15 (main) Hulton Archive/
Getty Images; p. 15 (Billy the Kid) http://commons.wikimedia.org/wiki/File:Billy_the_Kid_
tintype,_Fort_Sumner,_1879-80-Edit2.jpg; p. 17 Archive Photos/Moviepix/Getty Images;
p. 19 aragami12345s/Shutterstock.com.

Printed in the United States of America

CPSIA compliance information: Batch #CW13GS: For further information contact Gareth Stevens, New York, New York at 1-800-542-2595.

CONTENTS

Wild Tales 4

Where and When. 6

Cowboys 8

Ranch Life 10

Cattle Drives 12

Outlaws 14

Lawmen 16

Native Americans. 18

Making Up the Wild West 20

Glossary. 22

For More Information. 23

Index 24

Words in the glossary appear in **bold** type the first time they are used in the text.

What do you think of when you hear the words "Wild West"? You likely imagine a lively time and place filled with cowboys, Indians, and gunfights between outlaws and lawmen. Danger waited around every corner. Something was always happening. Life was never dull or boring. It was wild!

That's the picture painted by movies, TV shows, and books. But the truth doesn't always match the stories. What was it really like to live in the Wild West? Keep reading to find out!

Did-You-Know?

In 1856, the US military brought camels to the West! The camels were used to pull heavy loads. They did this well, but they were sold in the 1860s. Wild camels were spotted for years afterward.

There was more to life in the Wild West than just gunfights.

WHERE AND WHEN

The Wild West was in the West, of course. But what part of the United States was considered the West? Some people say it's the western half of the country. Others say it covers two-thirds of the country—from the Mississippi River to the Pacific Ocean!

What time period do we mean when we talk about the Wild West? Most people say it started around 1850 and ended around 1900. Some even believe it continued until about 1920.

Did You Know?

Wild West outlaws were still robbing stagecoaches until 1916. The famous Wild West lawman Wyatt Earp lived until 1929.

Wyatt Earp

Wild West

Mississippi River

COWBOYS

The cowboy may be the best-known **symbol** of the Wild West. Stories present the cowboy as a brave, strong hero. And cowboys had to be brave and strong—their work was hard and dangerous.

In stories, cowboys are usually white men. In real life, many cowboys were Native American, African American, and Mexican. Mexican cowboys were called vaqueros (vah-KEHR-ohz). American cowboys learned much of what they needed to know from the vaqueros. They copied the vaqueros' **equipment** and language.

Did You Know?

The famous cowboy Nat Love was born a slave in Tennessee in 1854. He wrote a book about his life, titled *The Life and Adventures of Nat Love*, that was printed in 1907.

The cowboy hat came from the sombrero worn by vaqueros. "Buckaroo," another name for a cowboy, came from vaquero.

9

Cowboys worked from sunrise to sunset almost every day. They cared for sick and hurt cattle, helped cows have their babies, and searched for lost cattle. They made and mended equipment. Cowboys didn't do much for fun at the end of the day. They were so tired from work that they went to bed early.

Ranch life was lonely since ranches were far from towns. Doctors were also far away, so sick or hurt cowboys had to be their own doctor.

Did You Know?

About the only way a woman could be a cowboy was to wear men's clothing and pretend to be a man. But women on family ranches often did a cowboy's work.

From riding in a saddle all day to the house they slept in, a cowboy's life wasn't very comfortable.

CATTLE DRIVES

Each spring, Texas cowboys spent about 3 months on cattle drives, or trail drives. They herded cattle to Kansas to sell them. Cowboys rode all day and took turns at night watching the cattle. They ate beans, bacon, biscuits, and rice. They wore the same clothes every day.

Cowboys faced storms, range fires, cattle **rustlers**, and, sometimes, angry Native Americans. If cattle **stampeded**, cowboys had to ride ahead of them to stop them. Driving cattle was hard, dangerous work.

Did You Know?

Cowboys received $25 to $40 a month for a cattle drive. The work was so hard and the pay was so poor that most made only one drive before finding other work.

Cattle drives could be as long as 1,000 miles (1,609 km)!

13

OUTLAWS

Outlaws are among the Wild West's most famous characters. Jesse James and his brother, Frank, robbed banks and trains. Another outlaw killed Jesse in 1882, but Frank returned to the family farm and lived until 1915.

Billy the Kid's real name was William Henry McCarty. He changed it to William H. Bonney to hide from lawmen. He was wanted for murder and horse stealing. But Mexican farmers in New Mexico considered him a hero because he fought the white ranchers who had taken their land.

Did You Know?

Belle Starr was friends with outlaws and known as the "Bandit Queen." But the only crime it's certain she committed is stealing a horse.

Billy the Kid

Belle Starr, pictured here, probably had ties to many other outlaws including the Youngers and Jesse James.

LAWMEN

Lawmen such as Bat Masterson and Wyatt Earp were colorful characters who had many different jobs during their life. Besides being lawmen, both were buffalo hunters, gunfighters, and **gamblers**. And Wyatt was often in trouble with the law. He was said to have stolen money and horses.

Wyatt took part in the famous gunfight at the O.K. **Corral** in Tombstone, Arizona. Three outlaws in a gang called the Cowboys were killed. Some said Wyatt was a hero. Others said he was a murderer.

Did You Know?

In places with few lawmen, **vigilantes** hunted down people believed to have committed crimes. Vigilantes sometimes killed the people they caught without waiting for the crime to be proven.

This picture shows a scene from the 1957 movie Gunfight at O.K. Corral.

In Wild West stories, Native Americans are often the "bad guys." It's true there were many wars with Native Americans. But that isn't the whole story.

Native Americans had lived in the West for thousands of years. There were many different Indian nations with different ways of life. When the US government and settlers took their land, they fought back. They wanted to keep their people safe and continue their way of life. Instead, they lost and were forced to live on **reservations**.

Did You Know?

Reservations destroyed Native American society. A Nez Percé leader called Chief Joseph said, "You might as well expect the rivers to run backward as that any man who was born a free man should be contented when penned up."

Today, many Native Americans still live on reservations. They continue to honor customs begun hundreds of years ago.

19

MAKING UP THE WILD WEST

The imagined idea of the Wild West came from many places. Buffalo Bill's traveling Wild West show, started in 1883, had cowboys, Indians, and action-packed plays. Writers who had never seen the West made up tales that had wild, mean Native Americans and few African Americans, Mexicans, and women.

Later, movies showed a Wild West with brave heroes, evil outlaws, and continuous adventure. But the true story of the Wild West is more interesting than all the made-up stories!

Did You Know?

Wyatt Earp wanted to be considered a great hero. So he told many stories about his bravery and deeds that weren't true.

A Timeline of the Wild West

1848
- Discovery of gold in California begins wars with Native Americans in the West.

- US military brings camels to the West.

1856

1866
- The first cattle drive takes place.
- Jesse and Frank James rob their first bank.

- Former slave Nat Love heads to Kansas to become a cowboy.

1869

- The gunfight at the O.K. Corral takes place.

1875
1881
- Billy the Kid commits his first crime.

1882
- Jesse James is killed.

- Buffalo Bill's Wild West show begins.

1883

1885
- Cattle drives end.

- Bat Masterson and Nat Love die.

1921
- Wyatt Earp dies.

1929

corral: a pen for livestock

equipment: tools, clothing, and other items needed for a job

gambler: someone who plays games to win money

ranch: a large farm for raising cattle or horses

reservation: public land set aside for Native Americans to live on

rustler: someone who steals cattle

stagecoach: a closed, horse-drawn wagon used to carry people and mail

stampede: to run wildly in panic

symbol: something that stands for something else

vigilante: a member of a citizens' group organized to control crime but having no legal authority

FOR MORE INFORMATION

Books

Lassieur, Allison. *The Wild West: An Interactive History Adventure*. Mankato, MN: Capstone Press, 2009.

Murray, Stuart. *Wild West*. New York, NY: DK Publishing, 2005.

Sheinkin, Steve. *Which Way to the Wild West?* New York, NY: Roaring Book Press, 2009.

Websites

Cowboy Facts for Kids
www.ehow.com/info_8171301_cowboy-kids.html
Read some fun facts about cowboys and find links to projects and games.

Native American Facts for Kids
www.native-languages.org/kids.htm
Learn more about the many different Native American people of North America.

Wild Wild West
www.kidskonnect.com/subject-index/16-history/286-wild-wild-west.html
Read facts about the Wild West and find links to websites about famous people and events.

Publisher's note to educators and parents: Our editors have carefully reviewed these websites to ensure that they are suitable for students. Many websites change frequently, however, and we cannot guarantee that a site's future contents will continue to meet our high standards of quality and educational value. Be advised that students should be closely supervised whenever they access the Internet.

Index

African Americans 8, 20

Billy the Kid 14, 15, 21

Buffalo Bill 20, 21

camels 4, 21

cattle drives 12, 13, 21

Chief Joseph 18

cowboys 4, 7, 8, 10, 11, 12, 20, 21

Earp, Wyatt 6, 7, 16, 20, 21

gamblers 16

gunfights 4, 5, 16

Indians 4, 18, 20

James, Frank 14, 21

James, Jesse 14, 15, 21

lawmen 4, 14, 16

Love, Nat 8, 21

Masterson, Bat 16, 21

Mexicans 8, 14, 20

Native Americans 8, 12, 18, 19, 20, 21

O.K. Corral 16, 17, 21

outlaws 4, 6, 14, 15, 16, 20

ranches 10

reservations 18, 19

rustlers 12

Starr, Belle 14, 15

vaqueros 8, 9

vigilantes 16

Wild West show 20, 21

women 10, 20